JOKES
COMEDY NOTEBOOK
FEATURING JOKE BUILDER SYSTEM

Property of the Hilarious

- -

Fun & Freebies!
BadPermUnicorn.com
Funny Adult
Coloring Books & More!

Blah, blah, blah. MOST important....**Thank You for supporting our wacky side hustle!** Transforming nutty ideas into fun books is a blast. Enjoy!

JOKE BUILDER

Topic _____ **Name**

Source ⠿ *True*   ⠿ *News*   ⠿ *Friend*   ⠿ *Fiction*

Main Frame

Main talking points for base story/frame. Essential facts only.

Mash-Up

Overlay unrelated topics for comedic effect. Contrast & exaggerate.
Make connections to different ideas. Weird works. Ridiculous rocks!

Brainstorm

Start writing. No editing/judgement (that's later). Don't force the funny.
Let the creative flow. Personalize facts. Set a timer for 5-10 min. Go!

Piece together funny words, situations, thoughts & questions from Brainstorm. Keep first draft under 250 words.

Joke Construction

_____
_____
_____
_____
_____
_____
_____
_____
_____
_____
_____
_____
_____
_____
_____

Fine-Tune the Funny Cut anything that doesn't serve the payoff. If it slows the show...it goes! Focus on flow.

_____
_____
_____
_____
_____
_____
_____
_____
_____
_____
_____
_____

JOKE BUILDER

Topic _____ **Name**

Source ⠿ *True*　　⠿ *News*　　⠿ *Friend*　　⠿ *Fiction*

Main Frame

Main talking points for base story/frame. Essential facts only.

Mash-Up

Overlay unrelated topics for comedic effect. Contrast & exaggerate.
Make connections to different ideas. Weird works. Ridiculous rocks!

Brainstorm

Start writing. No editing/judgement (that's later). Don't force the funny.
Let the creative flow. Personalize facts. Set a timer for 5-10 min. Go!

Piece together funny words, situations, thoughts & questions from Brainstorm. Keep first draft under 250 words.

Joke Construction

_____
_____
_____
_____
_____
_____
_____
_____
_____
_____
_____
_____
_____
_____
_____

Fine-Tune the Funny Cut anything that doesn't serve the payoff. If it slows the show...it goes! Focus on flow.

_____
_____
_____
_____
_____
_____
_____
_____
_____
_____
_____
_____

JOKE BUILDER

Topic

Name

Source ⠿ *True* ⠿ *News* ⠿ *Friend* ⠿ *Fiction*

Main Frame

Main talking points for base story/frame. Essential facts only

Mash-Up

Overlay unrelated topics for comedic effect. Contrast & exaggerate
Make connections to different ideas. Weird works. Ridiculous rocks

Brainstorm

Start writing. No editing/judgement (that's later). Don't force the funn
Let the creative flow. Personalize facts. Set a timer for 5-10 min. G

Piece together funny words, situations, thoughts & questions from Brainstorm. Keep first draft under 250 words.

Joke Construction

Fine-Tune the Funny Cut anything that doesn't serve the payoff. If it slows the show...it goes! Focus on flow.

JOKE BUILDER

Topic _____ **Name**

Source ⠿ *True*   ⠿ *News*   ⠿ *Friend*   ⠿ *Fiction*

Main Frame

Main talking points for base story/frame. Essential facts only.

Mash-Up

Overlay unrelated topics for comedic effect. Contrast & exaggerate.
Make connections to different ideas. Weird works. Ridiculous rocks!

Brainstorm

Start writing. No editing/judgement (that's later). Don't force the funny.
Let the creative flow. Personalize facts. Set a timer for 5-10 min. Go!

Piece together funny words, situations, thoughts & questions from Brainstorm. Keep first draft under 250 words.

Fine-Tune the Funny Cut anything that doesn't serve the payoff. If it slows the show...it goes! Focus on flow.

JOKE BUILDER

Topic _____ **Name**

Source ⠿ *True*   ⠿ *News*   ⠿ *Friend*   ⠿ *Fiction*

Main Frame

Main talking points for base story/frame. Essential facts only.

Mash-Up

Overlay unrelated topics for comedic effect. Contrast & exaggerate.
Make connections to different ideas. Weird works. Ridiculous rocks!

Brainstorm

Start writing. No editing/judgement (that's later). Don't force the funny.
Let the creative flow. Personalize facts. Set a timer for 5-10 min. Go!

Piece together funny words, situations, thoughts & questions from Brainstorm. Keep first draft under 250 words.

Joke Construction

_____
_____
_____
_____
_____
_____
_____
_____
_____
_____
_____
_____
_____
_____

Fine-Tune the Funny Cut anything that doesn't serve the payoff. If it slows the show...it goes! Focus on flow.

_____
_____
_____
_____
_____
_____
_____
_____
_____
_____
_____

JOKE BUILDER

Topic   **Name**

Source   ⫶ *True*   ⫶ *News*   ⫶ *Friend*   ⫶ *Fiction*

Main Frame

Main talking points for base story/frame. Essential facts only

Mash-Up

Overlay unrelated topics for comedic effect. Contrast & exaggerate
Make connections to different ideas. Weird works. Ridiculous rocks

Brainstorm

Start writing. No editing/judgement (that's later). Don't force the funny
Let the creative flow. Personalize facts. Set a timer for 5-10 min. G

Piece together funny words, situations, thoughts & questions from Brainstorm. Keep first draft under 250 words.

Joke Construction

Fine-Tune the Funny

Cut anything that doesn't serve the payoff. If it slows the show...it goes! Focus on flow.

JOKE BUILDER

Topic

Name

Source ⠇ *True* ⠇ *News* ⠇ *Friend* ⠇ *Fiction*

Main Frame

Main talking points for base story/frame. Essential facts only.

Mash-Up

Overlay unrelated topics for comedic effect. Contrast & exaggerate.
Make connections to different ideas. Weird works. Ridiculous rocks!

Brainstorm

Start writing. No editing/judgement (that's later). Don't force the funny
Let the creative flow. Personalize facts. Set a timer for 5-10 min. Go!

Piece together funny words, situations, thoughts & questions from Brainstorm. Keep first draft under 250 words.

Joke Construction

Fine-Tune the Funny

Cut anything that doesn't serve the payoff. If it slows the show...it goes! Focus on flow.

JOKE BUILDER

Topic

Name

Source ⋮⋮ *True*   ⋮⋮ *News*   ⋮⋮ *Friend*   ⋮⋮ *Fiction*

Main Frame

Main talking points for base story/frame. Essential facts only.

Mash-Up

Overlay unrelated topics for comedic effect. Contrast & exaggerate.
Make connections to different ideas. Weird works. Ridiculous rocks!

Brainstorm

Start writing. No editing/judgement (that's later). Don't force the funny.
Let the creative flow. Personalize facts. Set a timer for 5-10 min. Go!

Piece together funny words, situations, thoughts & questions from Brainstorm. Keep first draft under 250 words.

_____
_____
_____
_____
_____
_____
_____
_____
_____
_____
_____
_____
_____
_____

Fine-Tune the Funny Cut anything that doesn't serve the payoff. If it slows the show...it goes! Focus on flow.

_____
_____
_____
_____
_____
_____
_____
_____
_____
_____
_____
_____

JOKE BUILDER

Topic

Name

Source ⋮⋮ *True*   ⋮⋮ *News*   ⋮⋮ *Friend*   ⋮⋮ *Fiction*

Main Frame

Main talking points for base story/frame. Essential facts only

Mash-Up

Overlay unrelated topics for comedic effect. Contrast & exaggerate
Make connections to different ideas. Weird works. Ridiculous rocks

Brainstorm

Start writing. No editing/judgement (that's later). Don't force the funn
Let the creative flow. Personalize facts. Set a timer for 5-10 min. G

Piece together funny words, situations, thoughts & questions from Brainstorm. Keep first draft under 250 words.

Fine-Tune the Funny Cut anything that doesn't serve the payoff. If it slows the show...it goes! Focus on flow.

JOKE BUILDER

Topic   **Name**

Source   ⋮⋮ *True*   ⋮⋮ *News*   ⋮⋮ *Friend*   ⋮⋮ *Fiction*

Main Frame

Main talking points for base story/frame. Essential facts only.

Mash-Up

Overlay unrelated topics for comedic effect. Contrast & exaggerate.
Make connections to different ideas. Weird works. Ridiculous rocks!

Brainstorm

Start writing. No editing/judgement (that's later). Don't force the funny
Let the creative flow. Personalize facts. Set a timer for 5-10 min. Go

Piece together funny words, situations, thoughts & questions from Brainstorm. Keep first draft under 250 words.

Joke Construction

Fine-Tune the Funny

Cut anything that doesn't serve the payoff. If it slows the show...it goes! Focus on flow.

JOKE BUILDER

Topic _____ **Name**

Source ::: *True*   ::: *News*   ::: *Friend*   ::: *Fiction*

Main Frame

Main talking points for base story/frame. Essential facts only.

Mash-Up

Overlay unrelated topics for comedic effect. Contrast & exaggerate.
Make connections to different ideas. Weird works. Ridiculous rocks!

Brainstorm

Start writing. No editing/judgement (that's later). Don't force the funny.
Let the creative flow. Personalize facts. Set a timer for 5-10 min. Go!

Piece together funny words, situations, thoughts & questions from Brainstorm. Keep first draft under 250 words.

_____

_____

_____

_____

_____

_____

_____

_____

_____

_____

_____

_____

_____

Fine-Tune the Funny Cut anything that doesn't serve the payoff. If it slows the show...it goes! Focus on flow.

_____

_____

_____

_____

_____

_____

_____

_____

_____

_____

_____

_____

JOKE BUILDER

Topic

Name

Source ::: *True*   ::: *News*   ::: *Friend*   ::: *Fiction*

Main Frame

Main talking points for base story/frame. Essential facts only.

Mash-Up

Overlay unrelated topics for comedic effect. Contrast & exaggerate.
Make connections to different ideas. Weird works. Ridiculous rocks.

Brainstorm

Start writing. No editing/judgement (that's later). Don't force the funny.
Let the creative flow. Personalize facts. Set a timer for 5-10 min. Go

Piece together funny words, situations, thoughts & questions from Brainstorm. Keep first draft under 250 words.

_____
_____
_____
_____
_____
_____
_____
_____
_____
_____
_____
_____
_____

Fine-Tune the Funny Cut anything that doesn't serve the payoff. If it slows the show...it goes! Focus on flow.

_____
_____
_____
_____
_____
_____
_____
_____
_____
_____
_____
_____

JOKE BUILDER

Topic _____ **Name**

Source ⋮⋮ *True*   ⋮⋮ *News*   ⋮⋮ *Friend*   ⋮⋮ *Fiction*

Main Frame

Main talking points for base story/frame. Essential facts only.

Mash-Up

Overlay unrelated topics for comedic effect. Contrast & exaggerate.
Make connections to different ideas. Weird works. Ridiculous rocks!

Brainstorm

Start writing. No editing/judgement (that's later). Don't force the funny.
Let the creative flow. Personalize facts. Set a timer for 5-10 min. Go

Piece together funny words, situations, thoughts & questions from Brainstorm. Keep first draft under 250 words.

Joke Construction

Fine-Tune the Funny

Cut anything that doesn't serve the payoff. If it slows the show...it goes! Focus on flow.

JOKE BUILDER

Topic _____ **Name** _____

Source ⋮⋮ *True*   ⋮⋮ *News*   ⋮⋮ *Friend*   ⋮⋮ *Fiction*

Main Frame

Main talking points for base story/frame. Essential facts only.

Mash-Up

Overlay unrelated topics for comedic effect. Contrast & exaggerate.
Make connections to different ideas. Weird works. Ridiculous rocks!

Brainstorm

Start writing. No editing/judgement (that's later). Don't force the funny.
Let the creative flow. Personalize facts. Set a timer for 5-10 min. Go!

Piece together funny words, situations, thoughts & questions from Brainstorm. Keep first draft under 250 words.

_____
_____
_____
_____
_____
_____
_____
_____
_____
_____
_____
_____

Fine-Tune the Funny   Cut anything that doesn't serve the payoff. If it slows the show...it goes! Focus on flow.

_____
_____
_____
_____
_____
_____
_____
_____
_____
_____
_____

JOKE BUILDER

Topic   **Name**

Source   ⋮⋮ *True*   ⋮⋮ *News*   ⋮⋮ *Friend*   ⋮⋮ *Fiction*

Main Frame

Main talking points for base story/frame. Essential facts only

Mash-Up

Overlay unrelated topics for comedic effect. Contrast & exaggerate
Make connections to different ideas. Weird works. Ridiculous rocks

Brainstorm

Start writing. No editing/judgement (that's later). Don't force the funny
Let the creative flow. Personalize facts. Set a timer for 5-10 min. Go

Piece together funny words, situations, thoughts & questions from Brainstorm. Keep first draft under 250 words.

Joke Construction

Fine-Tune the Funny
Cut anything that doesn't serve the payoff. If it slows the show...it goes! Focus on flow.

JOKE BUILDER

Topic   **Name**

Source   ⠿ *True*   ⠿ *News*   ⠿ *Friend*   ⠿ *Fiction*

Main Frame

Main talking points for base story/frame. Essential facts only.

Mash-Up

Overlay unrelated topics for comedic effect. Contrast & exaggerate.
Make connections to different ideas. Weird works. Ridiculous rocks!

Brainstorm

Start writing. No editing/judgement (that's later). Don't force the funny.
Let the creative flow. Personalize facts. Set a timer for 5-10 min. Go

Piece together funny words, situations, thoughts & questions from Brainstorm. Keep first draft under 250 words.

Joke Construction

Fine-Tune the Funny Cut anything that doesn't serve the payoff. If it slows the show...it goes! Focus on flow.

JOKE BUILDER

Topic _____ **Name**

Source ⋮⋮ _True_   ⋮⋮ _News_   ⋮⋮ _Friend_   ⋮⋮ _Fiction_

Main Frame

Main talking points for base story/frame. Essential facts only.

Mash-Up

Overlay unrelated topics for comedic effect. Contrast & exaggerate.
Make connections to different ideas. Weird works. Ridiculous rocks!

Brainstorm

Start writing. No editing/judgement (that's later). Don't force the funny.
Let the creative flow. Personalize facts. Set a timer for 5-10 min. Go!

Piece together funny words, situations, thoughts & questions from Brainstorm. Keep first draft under 250 words.

Joke Construction

_____
_____
_____
_____
_____
_____
_____
_____
_____
_____
_____
_____

Fine-Tune the Funny

Cut anything that doesn't serve the payoff. If it slows the show...it goes! Focus on flow.

_____
_____
_____
_____
_____
_____
_____
_____
_____
_____
_____
_____

JOKE BUILDER

Topic   **Name**

Source   ⠿ *True*   ⠿ *News*   ⠿ *Friend*   ⠿ *Fiction*

Main Frame

Main talking points for base story/frame. Essential facts only

Mash-Up

Overlay unrelated topics for comedic effect. Contrast & exaggerate
Make connections to different ideas. Weird works. Ridiculous rock

Brainstorm

Start writing. No editing/judgement (that's later). Don't force the fun
Let the creative flow. Personalize facts. Set a timer for 5-10 min. G

Piece together funny words, situations, thoughts & questions from Brainstorm. Keep first draft under 250 words.

Fine-Tune the Funny Cut anything that doesn't serve the payoff. If it slows the show...it goes! Focus on flow.

JOKE BUILDER

Topic _____ **Name**

Source ⋮⋮ _True_   ⋮⋮ _News_   ⋮⋮ _Friend_   ⋮⋮ _Fiction_

Main Frame

Main talking points for base story/frame. Essential facts only.

Mash-Up

Overlay unrelated topics for comedic effect. Contrast & exaggerate.
Make connections to different ideas. Weird works. Ridiculous rocks!

Brainstorm

Start writing. No editing/judgement (that's later). Don't force the funny.
Let the creative flow. Personalize facts. Set a timer for 5-10 min. Go

Piece together funny words, situations, thoughts & questions from Brainstorm. Keep first draft under 250 words.

Joke Construction

Fine-Tune the Funny Cut anything that doesn't serve the payoff. If it slows the show...it goes! Focus on flow.

JOKE BUILDER

Topic

Name

Source ::: *True*   ::: *News*   ::: *Friend*   ::: *Fiction*

Main Frame

Main talking points for base story/frame. Essential facts only.

Mash-Up

Overlay unrelated topics for comedic effect. Contrast & exaggerate.
Make connections to different ideas. Weird works. Ridiculous rocks!

Brainstorm

Start writing. No editing/judgement (that's later). Don't force the funny.
Let the creative flow. Personalize facts. Set a timer for 5-10 min. Go!

Piece together funny words, situations, thoughts & questions from Brainstorm. Keep first draft under 250 words.

_____
_____
_____
_____
_____
_____
_____
_____
_____
_____
_____
_____
_____

Fine-Tune the Funny Cut anything that doesn't serve the payoff. If it slows the show...it goes! Focus on flow.

_____
_____
_____
_____
_____
_____
_____
_____
_____
_____
_____
_____
_____

JOKE BUILDER

Topic

Name

Source ⠿ *True*   ⠿ *News*   ⠿ *Friend*   ⠿ *Fiction*

Main Frame

Main talking points for base story/frame. Essential facts only

Mash-Up

Overlay unrelated topics for comedic effect. Contrast & exaggerat
Make connections to different ideas. Weird works. Ridiculous rock

Brainstorm

Start writing. No editing/judgement (that's later). Don't force the fun
Let the creative flow. Personalize facts. Set a timer for 5-10 min. G

Piece together funny words, situations, thoughts & questions from Brainstorm. Keep first draft under 250 words.

Joke Construction

_____

_____

_____

_____

_____

_____

_____

_____

_____

_____

_____

_____

_____

Fine-Tune the Funny Cut anything that doesn't serve the payoff. If it slows the show...it goes! Focus on flow.

_____

_____

_____

_____

_____

_____

_____

_____

_____

_____

_____

_____

JOKE BUILDER

Topic _____ **Name**

Source ⠿ *True*   ⠿ *News*   ⠿ *Friend*   ⠿ *Fiction*

Main Frame

Main talking points for base story/frame. Essential facts only.

Mash-Up

Overlay unrelated topics for comedic effect. Contrast & exaggerate.
Make connections to different ideas. Weird works. Ridiculous rocks!

Brainstorm

Start writing. No editing/judgement (that's later). Don't force the funny.
Let the creative flow. Personalize facts. Set a timer for 5-10 min. Go

Piece together funny words, situations, thoughts & questions from Brainstorm. Keep first draft under 250 words.

Joke Construction

Fine-Tune the Funny Cut anything that doesn't serve the payoff. If it slows the show...it goes! Focus on flow.

JOKE BUILDER

Topic   **Name**

Source   ::: *True*   ::: *News*   ::: *Friend*   ::: *Fiction*

Main Frame

Main talking points for base story/frame. Essential facts only.

Mash-Up

Overlay unrelated topics for comedic effect. Contrast & exaggerate.
Make connections to different ideas. Weird works. Ridiculous rocks!

Brainstorm

Start writing. No editing/judgement (that's later). Don't force the funny.
Let the creative flow. Personalize facts. Set a timer for 5-10 min. Go!

Piece together funny words, situations, thoughts & questions from Brainstorm. Keep first draft under 250 words.

Joke Construction

_____
_____
_____
_____
_____
_____
_____
_____
_____
_____
_____
_____
_____

Fine-Tune the Funny Cut anything that doesn't serve the payoff. If it slows the show...it goes! Focus on flow.

_____
_____
_____
_____
_____
_____
_____
_____
_____
_____
_____

JOKE BUILDER

Topic   **Name**

Source   ::: *True*   ::: *News*   ::: *Friend*   ::: *Fiction*

Main Frame

Main talking points for base story/frame. Essential facts only

Mash-Up

Overlay unrelated topics for comedic effect. Contrast & exaggerate
Make connections to different ideas. Weird works. Ridiculous rocks

Brainstorm

Start writing. No editing/judgement (that's later). Don't force the fun
Let the creative flow. Personalize facts. Set a timer for 5-10 min. G

Piece together funny words, situations, thoughts & questions from Brainstorm. Keep first draft under 250 words.

Joke Construction

_____

_____

_____

_____

_____

_____

_____

_____

_____

_____

_____

_____

_____

Fine-Tune the Funny Cut anything that doesn't serve the payoff. If it slows the show...it goes! Focus on flow.

_____

_____

_____

_____

_____

_____

_____

_____

_____

_____

_____

_____

JOKE BUILDER

Topic   **Name**

Source ⋮⋮ *True*   ⋮⋮ *News*   ⋮⋮ *Friend*   ⋮⋮ *Fiction*

Main Frame

Main talking points for base story/frame. Essential facts only.

Mash-Up

Overlay unrelated topics for comedic effect. Contrast & exaggerate.
Make connections to different ideas. Weird works. Ridiculous rocks!

Brainstorm

Start writing. No editing/judgement (that's later). Don't force the funny.
Let the creative flow. Personalize facts. Set a timer for 5-10 min. Go

Piece together funny words, situations, thoughts & questions from Brainstorm. Keep first draft under 250 words.

Joke Construction

Fine-Tune the Funny Cut anything that doesn't serve the payoff. If it slows the show...it goes! Focus on flow.

JOKE BUILDER

Topic   **Name**

Source   ⠿ *True*   ⠿ *News*   ⠿ *Friend*   ⠿ *Fiction*

Main Frame

Main talking points for base story/frame. Essential facts only.

Mash-Up

Overlay unrelated topics for comedic effect. Contrast & exaggerate.
Make connections to different ideas. Weird works. Ridiculous rocks!

Brainstorm

Start writing. No editing/judgement (that's later). Don't force the funny.
Let the creative flow. Personalize facts. Set a timer for 5-10 min. Go!

Piece together funny words, situations, thoughts & questions from Brainstorm. Keep first draft under 250 words.

_____

_____

_____

_____

_____

_____

_____

_____

_____

_____

_____

_____

Fine-Tune the Funny Cut anything that doesn't serve the payoff. If it slows the show...it goes! Focus on flow.

_____

_____

_____

_____

_____

_____

_____

_____

_____

_____

_____

JOKE BUILDER

Topic

Name

Source ⋮ *True* ⋮ *News* ⋮ *Friend* ⋮ *Fiction*

Main Frame

Main talking points for base story/frame. Essential facts only

Mash-Up

Overlay unrelated topics for comedic effect. Contrast & exaggerat
Make connections to different ideas. Weird works. Ridiculous rock

Brainstorm

Start writing. No editing/judgement (that's later). Don't force the fun
Let the creative flow. Personalize facts. Set a timer for 5-10 min. C

Piece together funny words, situations, thoughts & questions from Brainstorm. Keep first draft under 250 words.

Joke Construction

_____
_____
_____
_____
_____
_____
_____
_____
_____
_____
_____
_____
_____
_____
_____

Fine-Tune the Funny Cut anything that doesn't serve the payoff. If it slows the show...it goes! Focus on flow.

_____
_____
_____
_____
_____
_____
_____
_____
_____
_____
_____
_____
_____
_____
_____

JOKE BUILDER

Topic   **Name**

Source   ⋮⋮ *True*   ⋮⋮ *News*   ⋮⋮ *Friend*   ⋮⋮ *Fiction*

Main Frame

Main talking points for base story/frame. Essential facts only.

Mash-Up

Overlay unrelated topics for comedic effect. Contrast & exaggerate.
Make connections to different ideas. Weird works. Ridiculous rocks!

Brainstorm

Start writing. No editing/judgement (that's later). Don't force the funny.
Let the creative flow. Personalize facts. Set a timer for 5-10 min. Go

Piece together funny words, situations, thoughts & questions from Brainstorm. Keep first draft under 250 words.

Joke Construction

Fine-Tune the Funny

Cut anything that doesn't serve the payoff. If it slows the show...it goes! Focus on flow.

JOKE BUILDER

Topic _____ **Name**

Source ⋮⋮ *True*   ⋮⋮ *News*   ⋮⋮ *Friend*   ⋮⋮ *Fiction*

Main Frame

Main talking points for base story/frame. Essential facts only.

Mash-Up

Overlay unrelated topics for comedic effect. Contrast & exaggerate.
Make connections to different ideas. Weird works. Ridiculous rocks!

Brainstorm

Start writing. No editing/judgement (that's later). Don't force the funny.
Let the creative flow. Personalize facts. Set a timer for 5-10 min. Go!

Piece together funny words, situations, thoughts & questions from Brainstorm. Keep first draft under 250 words.

Joke Construction

_____
_____
_____
_____
_____
_____
_____
_____
_____
_____
_____

Fine-Tune the Funny

Cut anything that doesn't serve the payoff. If it slows the show...it goes! Focus on flow.

_____
_____
_____
_____
_____
_____
_____
_____
_____
_____

JOKE BUILDER

Topic

Nam

Source ⋮⋮ *True* ⋮⋮ *News* ⋮⋮ *Friend* ⋮⋮ *Fiction*

Main Frame

Main talking points for base story/frame. Essential facts onl⟩

Mash-Up

Overlay unrelated topics for comedic effect. Contrast & exaggerat
Make connections to different ideas. Weird works. Ridiculous rock

Brainstorm

Start writing. No editing/judgement (that's later). Don't force the fun⟩
Let the creative flow. Personalize facts. Set a timer for 5-10 min. C

Piece together funny words, situations, thoughts & questions from Brainstorm. Keep first draft under 250 words.

Joke Construction

_____
_____
_____
_____
_____
_____
_____
_____
_____
_____
_____
_____
_____
_____

Fine-Tune the Funny Cut anything that doesn't serve the payoff. If it slows the show...it goes! Focus on flow.

_____
_____
_____
_____
_____
_____
_____
_____
_____
_____
_____
_____
_____
_____
_____

JOKE BUILDER

Topic   **Name**

Source   ⫶ *True*   ⫶ *News*   ⫶ *Friend*   ⫶ *Fiction*

Main Frame

Main talking points for base story/frame. Essential facts only.

Mash-Up

Overlay unrelated topics for comedic effect. Contrast & exaggerate.
Make connections to different ideas. Weird works. Ridiculous rocks!

Brainstorm

Start writing. No editing/judgement (that's later). Don't force the funny.
Let the creative flow. Personalize facts. Set a timer for 5-10 min. Go

Piece together funny words, situations, thoughts & questions from Brainstorm. Keep first draft under 250 words.

Joke Construction

Fine-Tune the Funny Cut anything that doesn't serve the payoff. If it slows the show...it goes! Focus on flow.

JOKE BUILDER

Topic _____ **Name**

Source ⋮⋮ *True*   ⋮⋮ *News*   ⋮⋮ *Friend*   ⋮⋮ *Fiction*

Main Frame

Main talking points for base story/frame. Essential facts only.

Mash-Up

Overlay unrelated topics for comedic effect. Contrast & exaggerate.
Make connections to different ideas. Weird works. Ridiculous rocks!

Brainstorm

Start writing. No editing/judgement (that's later). Don't force the funny
Let the creative flow. Personalize facts. Set a timer for 5-10 min. Go!

Piece together funny words, situations, thoughts & questions from Brainstorm. Keep first draft under 250 words.

Joke Construction

_____

_____

_____

_____

_____

_____

_____

_____

_____

_____

_____

_____

_____

Fine-Tune the Funny Cut anything that doesn't serve the payoff. If it slows the show...it goes! Focus on flow.

_____

_____

_____

_____

_____

_____

_____

_____

_____

_____

_____

JOKE BUILDER

Topic   **Name**

Source   ⋮⋮ *True*   ⋮⋮ *News*   ⋮⋮ *Friend*   ⋮⋮ *Fiction*

Main Frame

Main talking points for base story/frame. Essential facts onl

Mash-Up

Overlay unrelated topics for comedic effect. Contrast & exaggerat
Make connections to different ideas. Weird works. Ridiculous rock

Brainstorm

Start writing. No editing/judgement (that's later). Don't force the fun
Let the creative flow. Personalize facts. Set a timer for 5-10 min. C

Piece together funny words, situations, thoughts & questions from Brainstorm. Keep first draft under 250 words.

Joke Construction

_____
_____
_____
_____
_____
_____
_____
_____
_____
_____
_____
_____
_____

Fine-Tune the Funny Cut anything that doesn't serve the payoff. If it slows the show...it goes! Focus on flow.

_____
_____
_____
_____
_____
_____
_____
_____
_____
_____
_____
_____
_____

JOKE BUILDER

Topic   **Name**

Source ⋮⋮ *True*   ⋮⋮ *News*   ⋮⋮ *Friend*   ⋮⋮ *Fiction*

Main Frame

Main talking points for base story/frame. Essential facts only.

Mash-Up

Overlay unrelated topics for comedic effect. Contrast & exaggerate.
Make connections to different ideas. Weird works. Ridiculous rocks!

Brainstorm

Start writing. No editing/judgement (that's later). Don't force the funny.
Let the creative flow. Personalize facts. Set a timer for 5-10 min. Go

Piece together funny words, situations, thoughts & questions from Brainstorm. Keep first draft under 250 words.

Joke Construction

Fine-Tune the Funny

Cut anything that doesn't serve the payoff. If it slows the show...it goes! Focus on flow.

JOKE BUILDER

Topic _____ **Name**

Source ⋮⋮ *True* ⋮⋮ *News* ⋮⋮ *Friend* ⋮⋮ *Fiction*

Main Frame

Main talking points for base story/frame. Essential facts only.

Mash-Up

Overlay unrelated topics for comedic effect. Contrast & exaggerate.
Make connections to different ideas. Weird works. Ridiculous rocks!

Brainstorm

Start writing. No editing/judgement (that's later). Don't force the funny
Let the creative flow. Personalize facts. Set a timer for 5-10 min. Go

Piece together funny words, situations, thoughts & questions from Brainstorm. Keep first draft under 250 words.

Joke Construction

_____

_____

_____

_____

_____

_____

_____

_____

_____

_____

_____

_____

_____

_____

_____

Fine-Tune the Funny Cut anything that doesn't serve the payoff. If it slows the show...it goes! Focus on flow.

_____

_____

_____

_____

_____

_____

_____

_____

_____

_____

_____

_____

JOKE BUILDER

Topic _____ **Nam**

Source ⠿ _True_   ⠿ _News_   ⠿ _Friend_   ⠿ _Fiction_

Main Frame

Main talking points for base story/frame. Essential facts onl·

Mash-Up

Overlay unrelated topics for comedic effect. Contrast & exaggerat
Make connections to different ideas. Weird works. Ridiculous rock

Brainstorm

Start writing. No editing/judgement (that's later). Don't force the fun
Let the creative flow. Personalize facts. Set a timer for 5-10 min. C

Piece together funny words, situations, thoughts & questions from Brainstorm. Keep first draft under 250 words.

Joke Construction

Fine-Tune the Funny
Cut anything that doesn't serve the payoff. If it slows the show...it goes! Focus on flow.

JOKE BUILDER

Topic   **Name**

Source   ::: *True*   ::: *News*   ::: *Friend*   ::: *Fiction*

Main Frame

Main talking points for base story/frame. Essential facts only.

Mash-Up

Overlay unrelated topics for comedic effect. Contrast & exaggerate
Make connections to different ideas. Weird works. Ridiculous rocks!

Brainstorm

Start writing. No editing/judgement (that's later). Don't force the funny
Let the creative flow. Personalize facts. Set a timer for 5-10 min. Go

Piece together funny words, situations, thoughts & questions from Brainstorm. Keep first draft under 250 words.

Joke Construction

Fine-Tune the Funny Cut anything that doesn't serve the payoff. If it slows the show...it goes! Focus on flow.

JOKE BUILDER

Topic _____ **Name**

Source   ⠿ _True_   ⠿ _News_   ⠿ _Friend_   ⠿ _Fiction_

Main Frame

Main talking points for base story/frame. Essential facts only.

Mash-Up

Overlay unrelated topics for comedic effect. Contrast & exaggerate.
Make connections to different ideas. Weird works. Ridiculous rocks!

Brainstorm

Start writing. No editing/judgement (that's later). Don't force the funny
Let the creative flow. Personalize facts. Set a timer for 5-10 min. Go

Piece together funny words, situations, thoughts & questions from Brainstorm. Keep first draft under 250 words.

Joke Construction

_____
_____
_____
_____
_____
_____
_____
_____
_____
_____
_____
_____
_____

Fine-Tune the Funny

Cut anything that doesn't serve the payoff. If it slows the show...it goes! Focus on flow.

_____
_____
_____
_____
_____
_____
_____
_____
_____
_____
_____
_____

JOKE BUILDER

Topic _____ **Nam**

Source ⠿ _True_   ⠿ _News_   ⠿ _Friend_   ⠿ _Fiction_

Main Frame

Main talking points for base story/frame. Essential facts onl

Mash-Up

Overlay unrelated topics for comedic effect. Contrast & exaggerat
Make connections to different ideas. Weird works. Ridiculous rock

Brainstorm

Start writing. No editing/judgement (that's later). Don't force the fun
Let the creative flow. Personalize facts. Set a timer for 5-10 min. C

Piece together funny words, situations, thoughts & questions from Brainstorm. Keep first draft under 250 words.

Joke Construction

_____
_____
_____
_____
_____
_____
_____
_____
_____
_____
_____
_____
_____
_____
_____

Fine-Tune the Funny Cut anything that doesn't serve the payoff. If it slows the show...it goes! Focus on flow.

_____
_____
_____
_____
_____
_____
_____
_____
_____
_____
_____
_____
_____
_____

JOKE BUILDER

Topic   **Name**

Source   ⋮⋮⋮ *True*   ⋮⋮⋮ *News*   ⋮⋮⋮ *Friend*   ⋮⋮⋮ *Fiction*

Main Frame

Main talking points for base story/frame. Essential facts only.

Mash-Up

Overlay unrelated topics for comedic effect. Contrast & exaggerate
Make connections to different ideas. Weird works. Ridiculous rocks

Brainstorm

Start writing. No editing/judgement (that's later). Don't force the funny
Let the creative flow. Personalize facts. Set a timer for 5-10 min. Go

Piece together funny words, situations, thoughts & questions from Brainstorm. Keep first draft under 250 words.

Joke Construction

Fine-Tune the Funny

Cut anything that doesn't serve the payoff. If it slows the show...it goes! Focus on flow.

JOKE BUILDER

Topic _____ **Name**

Source ⠿ *True*   ⠿ *News*   ⠿ *Friend*   ⠿ *Fiction*

Main Frame

Main talking points for base story/frame. Essential facts only.

Mash-Up

Overlay unrelated topics for comedic effect. Contrast & exaggerate.
Make connections to different ideas. Weird works. Ridiculous rocks!

Brainstorm

Start writing. No editing/judgement (that's later). Don't force the funny.
Let the creative flow. Personalize facts. Set a timer for 5-10 min. Go

Piece together funny words, situations, thoughts & questions from Brainstorm. Keep first draft under 250 words.

_____

_____

_____

_____

_____

_____

_____

_____

_____

_____

_____

_____

_____

Fine-Tune the Funny Cut anything that doesn't serve the payoff. If it slows the show...it goes! Focus on flow.

_____

_____

_____

_____

_____

_____

_____

_____

_____

_____

_____

_____

JOKE BUILDER

Topic   **Nam**

Source ::: *True*   ::: *News*   ::: *Friend*   ::: *Fiction*

Main Frame

Main talking points for base story/frame. Essential facts on

Mash-Up

Overlay unrelated topics for comedic effect. Contrast & exaggerat
Make connections to different ideas. Weird works. Ridiculous rock

Brainstorm

Start writing. No editing/judgement (that's later). Don't force the fun
Let the creative flow. Personalize facts. Set a timer for 5-10 min. C

Piece together funny words, situations, thoughts & questions from Brainstorm. Keep first draft under 250 words.

Joke Construction

_____

_____

_____

_____

_____

_____

_____

_____

_____

_____

_____

_____

_____

_____

Fine-Tune the Funny

Cut anything that doesn't serve the payoff. If it slows the show...it goes! Focus on flow.

_____

_____

_____

_____

_____

_____

_____

_____

_____

_____

_____

_____

JOKE BUILDER

Topic _____ **Name**

Source ⠿ *True*   ⠿ *News*   ⠿ *Friend*   ⠿ *Fiction*

Main Frame

Main talking points for base story/frame. Essential facts only.

Mash-Up

Overlay unrelated topics for comedic effect. Contrast & exaggerate
Make connections to different ideas. Weird works. Ridiculous rocks!

Brainstorm

Start writing. No editing/judgement (that's later). Don't force the funny
Let the creative flow. Personalize facts. Set a timer for 5-10 min. Go

Piece together funny words, situations, thoughts & questions from Brainstorm. Keep first draft under 250 words.

Joke Construction

Fine-Tune the Funny Cut anything that doesn't serve the payoff. If it slows the show...it goes! Focus on flow.

JOKE BUILDER

Topic _____ **Name** _____

Source ::: *True*   ::: *News*   ::: *Friend*   ::: *Fiction*

Main Frame

Main talking points for base story/frame. Essential facts only.

Mash-Up

Overlay unrelated topics for comedic effect. Contrast & exaggerate.
Make connections to different ideas. Weird works. Ridiculous rocks!

Brainstorm

Start writing. No editing/judgement (that's later). Don't force the funny
Let the creative flow. Personalize facts. Set a timer for 5-10 min. Go

Piece together funny words, situations, thoughts & questions from Brainstorm. Keep first draft under 250 words.

Joke Construction

_____
_____
_____
_____
_____
_____
_____
_____
_____
_____
_____
_____
_____

Fine-Tune the Funny

Cut anything that doesn't serve the payoff. If it slows the show...it goes! Focus on flow.

_____
_____
_____
_____
_____
_____
_____
_____
_____
_____
_____

JOKE BUILDER

Topic

Nam

Source   ::: *True*   ::: *News*   ::: *Friend*   ::: *Fiction*

Main Frame

Main talking points for base story/frame. Essential facts onl

Mash-Up

Overlay unrelated topics for comedic effect. Contrast & exaggerat
Make connections to different ideas. Weird works. Ridiculous rock

Brainstorm

Start writing. No editing/judgement (that's later). Don't force the fun
Let the creative flow. Personalize facts. Set a timer for 5-10 min. C

Piece together funny words, situations, thoughts & questions from Brainstorm. Keep first draft under 250 words.

_____
_____
_____
_____
_____
_____
_____
_____
_____
_____
_____
_____
_____
_____

Fine-Tune the Funny Cut anything that doesn't serve the payoff. If it slows the show...it goes! Focus on flow.

_____
_____
_____
_____
_____
_____
_____
_____
_____
_____
_____
_____
_____
_____
_____

JOKE BUILDER

Topic   **Name**

Source ::: *True*   ::: *News*   ::: *Friend*   ::: *Fiction*

Main Frame

Main talking points for base story/frame. Essential facts only.

Mash-Up

Overlay unrelated topics for comedic effect. Contrast & exaggerate
Make connections to different ideas. Weird works. Ridiculous rocks

Brainstorm

Start writing. No editing/judgement (that's later). Don't force the funn
Let the creative flow. Personalize facts. Set a timer for 5-10 min. Go

Piece together funny words, situations, thoughts & questions from Brainstorm. Keep first draft under 250 words.

Joke Construction

Fine-Tune the Funny Cut anything that doesn't serve the payoff. If it slows the show...it goes! Focus on flow.

JOKE BUILDER

Topic   **Name**

Source ∴ *True*   ∴ *News*   ∴ *Friend*   ∴ *Fiction*

Main Frame

Main talking points for base story/frame. Essential facts only.

Mash-Up

Overlay unrelated topics for comedic effect. Contrast & exaggerate.
Make connections to different ideas. Weird works. Ridiculous rocks!

Brainstorm

Start writing. No editing/judgement (that's later). Don't force the funny.
Let the creative flow. Personalize facts. Set a timer for 5-10 min. Go

Piece together funny words, situations, thoughts & questions from Brainstorm. Keep first draft under 250 words.

Joke Construction

Fine-Tune the Funny Cut anything that doesn't serve the payoff. If it slows the show...it goes! Focus on flow.

JOKE BUILDER

Topic | **Nam**

Source ::: *True*   ::: *News*   ::: *Friend*   ::: *Fiction*

Main Frame

Main talking points for base story/frame. Essential facts onl

Mash-Up

Overlay unrelated topics for comedic effect. Contrast & exaggera
Make connections to different ideas. Weird works. Ridiculous rock

Brainstorm

Start writing. No editing/judgement (that's later). Don't force the fun
Let the creative flow. Personalize facts. Set a timer for 5-10 min. C

Piece together funny words, situations, thoughts & questions from Brainstorm. Keep first draft under 250 words.

Joke Construction

_____
_____
_____
_____
_____
_____
_____
_____
_____
_____
_____
_____
_____
_____

Fine-Tune the Funny

Cut anything that doesn't serve the payoff. If it slows the show...it goes! Focus on flow.

_____
_____
_____
_____
_____
_____
_____
_____
_____
_____
_____
_____

JOKE BUILDER

Topic   **Name**

Source   ⸭ *True*   ⸭ *News*   ⸭ *Friend*   ⸭ *Fiction*

Main Frame

Main talking points for base story/frame. Essential facts only.

Mash-Up

Overlay unrelated topics for comedic effect. Contrast & exaggerate
Make connections to different ideas. Weird works. Ridiculous rocks

Brainstorm

Start writing. No editing/judgement (that's later). Don't force the funn
Let the creative flow. Personalize facts. Set a timer for 5-10 min. Gc

Piece together funny words, situations, thoughts & questions from Brainstorm. Keep first draft under 250 words.

Joke Construction

Fine-Tune the Funny Cut anything that doesn't serve the payoff. If it slows the show...it goes! Focus on flow.

JOKE BUILDER

Topic   **Name**

Source   :·: *True*   :·: *News*   :·: *Friend*   :·: *Fiction*

Main Frame

Main talking points for base story/frame. Essential facts only.

Mash-Up

Overlay unrelated topics for comedic effect. Contrast & exaggerate.
Make connections to different ideas. Weird works. Ridiculous rocks!

Brainstorm

Start writing. No editing/judgement (that's later). Don't force the funny.
Let the creative flow. Personalize facts. Set a timer for 5-10 min. Go

Piece together funny words, situations, thoughts & questions from Brainstorm. Keep first draft under 250 words.

Joke Construction

_____
_____
_____
_____
_____
_____
_____
_____
_____
_____
_____
_____
_____

Fine-Tune the Funny

Cut anything that doesn't serve the payoff. If it slows the show...it goes! Focus on flow.

_____
_____
_____
_____
_____
_____
_____
_____
_____
_____

JOKE BUILDER

Topic

Nam

Source ⠿ *True*   ⠿ *News*   ⠿ *Friend*   ⠿ *Fiction*

Main Frame

Main talking points for base story/frame. Essential facts on▮

Mash-Up

Overlay unrelated topics for comedic effect. Contrast & exaggera▮
Make connections to different ideas. Weird works. Ridiculous roc▮

Brainstorm

Start writing. No editing/judgement (that's later). Don't force the fun▮
Let the creative flow. Personalize facts. Set a timer for 5-10 min. ◖

Piece together funny words, situations, thoughts & questions from Brainstorm. Keep first draft under 250 words.

Fine-Tune the Funny Cut anything that doesn't serve the payoff. If it slows the show...it goes! Focus on flow.

JOKE BUILDER

Topic _____ **Name**

Source ⠿ *True* ⠿ *News* ⠿ *Friend* ⠿ *Fiction*

Main Frame

Main talking points for base story/frame. Essential facts only.

Mash-Up

Overlay unrelated topics for comedic effect. Contrast & exaggerate
Make connections to different ideas. Weird works. Ridiculous rocks

Brainstorm

Start writing. No editing/judgement (that's later). Don't force the funny
Let the creative flow. Personalize facts. Set a timer for 5-10 min. Go

Piece together funny words, situations, thoughts & questions from Brainstorm. Keep first draft under 250 words.

Joke Construction

_____
_____
_____
_____
_____
_____
_____
_____
_____
_____
_____
_____
_____

Fine-Tune the Funny Cut anything that doesn't serve the payoff. If it slows the show...it goes! Focus on flow.

_____
_____
_____
_____
_____
_____
_____
_____
_____
_____

JOKE BUILDER

Topic _____ **Name**

Source ⋮⋮ *True*   ⋮⋮ *News*   ⋮⋮ *Friend*   ⋮⋮ *Fiction*

Main Frame

Main talking points for base story/frame. Essential facts only.

Mash-Up

Overlay unrelated topics for comedic effect. Contrast & exaggerate.
Make connections to different ideas. Weird works. Ridiculous rocks!

Brainstorm

Start writing. No editing/judgement (that's later). Don't force the funny.
Let the creative flow. Personalize facts. Set a timer for 5-10 min. Go

Piece together funny words, situations, thoughts & questions from Brainstorm. Keep first draft under 250 words.

Joke Construction

_____

_____

_____

_____

_____

_____

_____

_____

_____

_____

_____

_____

Fine-Tune the Funny

Cut anything that doesn't serve the payoff. If it slows the show...it goes! Focus on flow.

_____

_____

_____

_____

_____

_____

_____

_____

_____

_____

_____

Special Request

Your brief Amazon review could really help our family business. This link will take you to the Amazon.com review page for this book:

BadPermUnicorn.com/review42

Thank You!

Open Other End

Made in United States
North Haven, CT
27 November 2022

27401636R00065